Thriving with Borderline Personality Disorder

Proven Strategies for Managing Emotions, Building Resilience, and Living a Fulfilling Life

Emma Greenwood

CONTENTS

Introduction

Thriving Despite BPD

I sat on my bed, tears streaming down my face, feeling the familiar weight of an emotional storm. I had been here before, countless times—overwhelmed by the intensity of my feelings, unsure how to navigate the chaos within my mind. Diagnosed with Borderline Personality Disorder (BPD) in my early twenties, I had spent years grappling with mood swings, impulsive behaviors, and a profound fear of abandonment. The world saw me as "difficult" and "unstable," but I was determined to change my narrative.

My journey began with a crucial step: understanding my diagnosis. Borderline Personality Disorder is often misunderstood and stigmatized. People with BPD experience intense emotions, unstable relationships, and a fragile sense of self. For me, comprehending these symptoms didn't just provide a label; it offered me a roadmap for change.

Understanding BPD was like turning on a light in a dark room. Suddenly, the seemingly erratic and overwhelming emotions made sense. I learned that my brain processes emotions differently, leading to intense emotional reactions. This knowledge was empowering—it meant that I wasn't "crazy" or "broken," but rather, I had a condition that could be managed with the right strategies.

One of the pivotal moments in my journey was seeking professional help. I found a therapist who understood BPD and worked with me to develop coping strategies. Together, we explored dialectical behavior therapy (DBT), which focuses on building skills in mindfulness, distress tolerance, emotional regulation, and interpersonal effectiveness. Through

DBT, I learned how to manage my emotions, reduce self-destructive behaviors, and improve my relationships.

I realized that my intense emotions, while challenging, also allowed me to experience life more vividly. This emotional sensitivity, which I once saw as a curse, became my superpower. I felt deeply, loved passionately, and had a unique empathy for others. My ability to deeply connect with others led me to volunteer at a local crisis hotline. My experiences gave me the empathy and understanding needed to support others in their darkest moments. What was once my greatest struggle became a source of strength and purpose.

Building resilience was another critical aspect of my journey. I developed daily practices that helped me maintain emotional stability. Morning meditation, journaling, and physical exercise became my anchors. I started each day with a 10-minute meditation session. This simple practice helped me center myself and set a positive tone for the day. I also kept a journal where I reflected on my feelings and tracked my progress.

Isolation can exacerbate BPD symptoms, so I worked on building a support network. I joined a support group where I connected with others who understood my struggles. These relationships provided a sense of belonging and validation. My support group became my lifeline. Through shared experiences and mutual support, I found strength in the community. I also rebuilt relationships with family and friends by being open about my journey and setting healthy boundaries.

I learned to celebrate small victories. Every step forward, no matter how small, was a testament to my progress. These celebrations reinforced my sense of achievement and motivated me to keep going. I celebrated my one-month milestone of consistent journaling and meditation by treating myself to a day at the spa. Recognizing these small achievements helped me stay positive and motivated.

My story is one of many that show thriving with BPD is possible. With the right tools, support, and mindset, you too can transform your struggles into strengths. This book will guide you through proven strategies, inspiring stories, and actionable advice to help you thrive despite BPD.

As you embark on this journey, remember: change is possible, and you are not alone. The path to thriving with BPD is challenging but deeply rewarding. Let my story be a beacon of hope and inspiration as you take your first steps towards a fulfilling life.

PART I

Understanding Borderline Personality Disorder

CHAPTER 1

What is Borderline Personality Disorder?

Borderline Personality Disorder is a mental health condition characterized by pervasive instability in moods, behavior, self-image, and functioning. This instability often leads to impulsive actions and problems in relationships with others. People with BPD may experience intense episodes of anger, depression, and anxiety that can last from a few hours to a few days.

Imagine living in a world where your emotions feel like a rollercoaster, constantly shifting from one extreme to another. One moment, you might feel on top of the world, and the next, you're plunged into the depths of despair. This is the reality for many people with BPD, making it a challenging condition to navigate.

Symptoms and Diagnostic Criteria

Understanding the symptoms of BPD is crucial for identifying the condition and seeking appropriate help. The Diagnostic and Statistical Manual of Mental Disorders, Fifth Edition (DSM-5) outlines specific criteria for diagnosing BPD. Let's break down these symptoms in an accessible way:

1. **Fear of Abandonment:** A pervasive fear of being left alone or abandoned, often leading to frantic efforts to avoid real or imagined separation.

2. **Unstable Relationships:** Intense and unstable relationships characterized by alternating between idealization and devaluation.

3. **Unstable Self-Image:** A distorted and unstable self-image or sense of self.

4. **Impulsive Behaviors:** Impulsive actions in at least two areas that are potentially self-damaging, such as spending, sex, substance abuse, reckless driving, or binge eating.

5. **Emotional Instability:** Intense and rapidly changing moods, often triggered by external events.

6. **Chronic Feelings of Emptiness:** A persistent feeling of emptiness or boredom.

7. **Inappropriate Anger:** Intense anger or difficulty controlling anger, often followed by feelings of shame or guilt.

8. **Stress-Related Paranoia or Dissociation:** Transient, stress-related paranoid thoughts or severe dissociative symptoms.

Recognizing these symptoms can be the first step toward understanding and managing BPD. It's important to note that not everyone with BPD will experience all of these symptoms, and their intensity can vary from person to person.

<u>**Common Misconceptions and Myths**</u>

Despite increased awareness, many misconceptions about BPD still exist, contributing to stigma and misunderstanding. Let's debunk some of these myths and replace them with facts:

Myth 1: People with BPD are "manipulative."

<u>Fact:</u> While individuals with BPD may exhibit behaviors that appear manipulative, these actions are often desperate attempts to cope with overwhelming emotions and fears of abandonment. Understanding the underlying causes of these behaviors can foster empathy and support.

Myth 2: BPD is untreatable.

<u>Fact:</u> BPD is treatable, and many people with BPD improve significantly with the right therapy and support. Treatments such as Dialectical Behavior Therapy (DBT) and Cognitive Behavioral Therapy

(CBT) have proven effective in helping individuals manage their symptoms and lead fulfilling lives.

Myth 3: Only women have BPD.

<u>Fact:</u> BPD affects both men and women. While it is diagnosed more frequently in women, likely due to social and cultural factors, men are also affected but may be underdiagnosed or misdiagnosed with other conditions such as depression or PTSD.

Myth 4: People with BPD are always in crisis.

<u>Fact:</u> While individuals with BPD can experience intense emotions and crises, many lead stable and productive lives, especially with proper treatment and support. It's essential to see beyond the disorder and recognize the person's strengths and potential.

Myth 5: BPD is just "drama."

<u>Fact:</u> BPD is a serious mental health condition that causes real suffering. Dismissing it as drama

undermines the experiences of those affected and can prevent them from seeking the help they need.

By addressing these myths, we can create a more compassionate and informed perspective on BPD. Understanding that BPD is a complex, multifaceted condition is the first step toward supporting those who live with it. Throughout this book, we'll explore strategies and stories that highlight resilience, hope, and the possibility of thriving despite the challenges of BPD.

Remember, knowledge is power. The more we understand about BPD, the better equipped we are to manage it effectively and support those who are affected. Whether you're reading this book for yourself or a loved one, know that you're not alone on this journey. Together, we can navigate the complexities of BPD and move toward a brighter, more stable future.

CHAPTER 2

The Science Behind BPD

Understanding the science behind Borderline Personality Disorder (BPD) is crucial to demystifying this complex condition. As a self-help coach, I aim to break down the biological, psychological, and environmental factors that contribute to BPD and examine its impact on the brain and emotional regulation. By doing so, we can gain a comprehensive view of BPD that fosters empathy, understanding, and effective management.

Biological, Psychological, and Environmental Factors

Let's start by looking at the factors that contribute to the development of BPD. It's essential to recognize that BPD is a multifaceted disorder, arising from a combination of biological, psychological, and environmental influences.

Biological Factors:

Research suggests that genetics play a significant role in the development of BPD. If a close family member has BPD, there's a higher likelihood of developing the disorder. Studies have also identified structural and functional abnormalities in the brain, particularly in areas that regulate emotions and impulse control. For instance, the amygdala, which processes emotions, may be overactive, while the prefrontal cortex, responsible for decision-making and impulse control, may be underactive in individuals with BPD.

Psychological Factors:

Childhood experiences, particularly those involving trauma, abuse, or neglect, are strongly linked to BPD. These adverse experiences can disrupt the development of a stable sense of self and healthy coping mechanisms. Individuals with BPD often struggle with intense fear of abandonment and difficulties in managing emotions, stemming from these early psychological wounds.

Environmental Factors:

The environment in which one grows up also plays a critical role. Unstable or chaotic family dynamics, exposure to violence, and a lack of supportive relationships can exacerbate the risk of developing BPD. Conversely, positive influences such as supportive family members, stable friendships, and access to mental health resources can mitigate some of these risks.

The Impact of BPD on the Brain and Emotional Regulation

Brain Structure and Function:

As mentioned earlier, the amygdala and prefrontal cortex are key players in BPD. The amygdala's heightened activity means that individuals with BPD often have a heightened sensitivity to emotional stimuli. This can make everyday experiences feel overwhelmingly intense. On the other hand, the prefrontal cortex's reduced activity impairs the ability to regulate these intense emotions and impulses, leading to the characteristic mood swings and impulsive behaviors seen in BPD.

Neurotransmitters:

Neurotransmitters like serotonin, dopamine, and norepinephrine are crucial in mood regulation and emotional stability. Imbalances in these chemicals are commonly found in individuals with BPD. For instance, low levels of serotonin are associated with impulsivity and aggression, while dopamine dysregulation can contribute to mood instability and difficulties in processing rewards and punishments.

Emotional Regulation:

People with BPD often experience difficulties in emotional regulation, a process that involves recognizing, understanding, and managing emotions. This challenge is not a result of a lack of willpower or effort but is deeply rooted in the brain's functioning. The inability to regulate emotions effectively can lead to rapid shifts in mood, from intense anger and sadness to periods of anxiety and emptiness.

Latest Research and Findings

Recent research has provided new insights into BPD, offering hope for better understanding and treatment of the disorder.

Genetic Research:

Advancements in genetic research have identified specific genes that may increase the risk of developing BPD. These genes are involved in regulating emotions and stress responses. Understanding these genetic links can pave the way for more targeted therapies that address the biological underpinnings of BPD.

Brain Imaging Studies:

Functional and structural brain imaging studies have provided valuable insights into the neural mechanisms of BPD. For example, functional MRI (fMRI) scans have shown that individuals with BPD have increased activity in the amygdala in response to emotional stimuli and reduced activity in the prefrontal cortex during tasks requiring impulse control. These findings highlight the importance of therapies that focus on emotion regulation and impulse control.

Therapeutic Approaches:

Innovative therapeutic approaches are being developed and tested. Dialectical Behavior Therapy

(DBT), originally created by Dr. Marsha Linehan, remains one of the most effective treatments for BPD. DBT combines cognitive-behavioral techniques with mindfulness practices to help individuals manage their emotions, reduce self-destructive behaviors, and improve relationships. Recent adaptations of DBT are being tailored to better meet the needs of diverse populations.

Pharmacological Advances:

While there is no specific medication for BPD, ongoing research is exploring the potential benefits of pharmacological treatments to manage symptoms. Medications that target neurotransmitter imbalances, such as mood stabilizers and antipsychotics, are being studied for their effectiveness in reducing mood swings, impulsivity, and aggression.

Early Intervention:

There is growing evidence that early intervention can significantly improve outcomes for individuals with BPD. Identifying and addressing symptoms during adolescence or early adulthood can prevent the disorder from becoming more severe. Programs that focus on building emotional regulation skills, resilience, and healthy relationships in young people are showing promising results.

Understanding the science behind Borderline Personality Disorder is a crucial step in demystifying this complex condition and fostering empathy and effective management strategies. By exploring the biological, psychological, and environmental factors, examining the impact on the brain and emotional regulation, and staying informed about the latest research and findings, we can better support those affected by BPD.

Remember, knowledge is a powerful tool. Whether you are seeking to understand your own experiences or support a loved one with BPD, gaining insights into the science behind the disorder can empower you to take proactive steps toward healing and growth. As we continue this journey together, I encourage you to stay curious, compassionate, and committed to the path of understanding and resilience.

PART II

Managing Emotions

CHAPTER 3

Emotional Awareness

Imagine waking up in the morning with a heavy feeling in your chest. You're not sure why, but you feel uneasy, anxious, or maybe even sad. Throughout the day, this feeling affects your interactions, your decisions, and your overall sense of well-being. This is a common experience for many people with Borderline Personality Disorder (BPD), but the good news is that developing emotional awareness can help manage these intense emotions. As a self-help coach, I am here to guide you through techniques for identifying and understanding your emotions and to highlight the role of mindfulness in achieving emotional awareness.

Techniques for Identifying and Understanding Emotions

The first step in managing emotions is to identify and understand them. This might seem straightforward, but for many people with BPD, emotions can be overwhelming and difficult to pinpoint. Here are some effective techniques to help you become more aware of your emotional landscape:

1. Emotion Journaling:

Keeping a journal where you regularly record your emotions can be incredibly insightful. Start by noting down what you're feeling at different times of the day. Describe the emotion in as much detail as possible. Are you feeling angry, sad, anxious, or happy? Try to go deeper by asking yourself why you might be feeling this way. What triggered this emotion? Journaling can help you recognize patterns in your emotional responses and gain clarity on what affects your mood.

2. Emotion Labeling:

Sometimes, just putting a name to what you're feeling can make a huge difference. When you experience an emotion, take a moment to label it. Say to yourself, "I am feeling frustrated," or "I am feeling excited." This simple act of naming the emotion can create a small distance between you and the feeling, allowing you to observe it more objectively.

3. Physical Sensations:

Emotions are often accompanied by physical sensations. Pay attention to how your body reacts when you experience different emotions. For instance, anxiety might come with a racing heart, sweaty palms, or a tight chest. Sadness might manifest as a heaviness in your limbs or a lump in your throat. By tuning into these physical cues, you can become more attuned to your emotional state.

4. Thought Patterns:

Emotions and thoughts are closely linked. Notice the thoughts that accompany your emotions. Are you thinking self-critical thoughts when you're feeling down? Are you having catastrophic thoughts when you're anxious? Identifying these thought patterns can help you understand the roots of your emotions and work towards changing unhelpful thinking habits.

5. Emotional Triggers:

Identify the situations, people, or events that trigger strong emotional reactions. This can be challenging but incredibly valuable. Knowing your triggers allows you to anticipate and prepare for emotional responses, giving you more control over how you handle them.

The Role of Mindfulness in Emotional Awareness

Mindfulness is a powerful tool for developing emotional awareness. It involves paying attention to the present moment without judgment. When practiced regularly, mindfulness can help you observe your emotions as they arise and respond to them in a more balanced way.

1. Mindful Breathing:

One of the simplest mindfulness techniques is mindful breathing. Whenever you feel overwhelmed by emotions, take a few moments to focus on your breath. Breathe in slowly through your nose, hold for a few seconds, and then exhale through your mouth. Concentrating on your breath helps anchor you in the present moment and creates a pause between the emotion and your reaction.

2. Body Scan Meditation:

A body scan meditation involves mentally scanning your body from head to toe, noticing any sensations without trying to change them. This practice helps you become more aware of the physical manifestations of your emotions. Find a quiet place to sit or lie down, close your eyes, and slowly bring your attention to different parts of your body. Notice any areas of tension, relaxation, warmth, or discomfort. This exercise can help you connect your physical sensations with your emotional state.

3. Observing Thoughts:

In mindfulness practice, it's important to observe your thoughts without getting caught up in them. Imagine your thoughts are like clouds passing through the sky or leaves floating down a stream. Watch them come and go without attaching any judgment or emotion to them. This technique can help you distance yourself from your emotions and see them more clearly.

4. Mindful Activities:

Incorporate mindfulness into your daily activities. Whether you're eating, walking, or even washing dishes, focus on the sensations, smells, sounds, and sights around you. By being fully present in these activities, you can practice mindfulness and enhance your emotional awareness.

5. Compassionate Self-Reflection:

Mindfulness also involves cultivating compassion towards yourself. When you notice a difficult emotion, instead of judging yourself for feeling it, offer yourself kindness and understanding. Say to yourself, "It's okay to feel this way. Emotions are a natural part of being human." This self-compassionate approach can reduce the intensity of negative emotions and help you respond to them more effectively.

Developing emotional awareness is a crucial step in managing the intense emotions associated with BPD. By using techniques like emotion journaling, labeling, and mindfulness practices, you can gain a deeper understanding of your emotional landscape. This understanding empowers you to respond to your emotions with greater clarity and control, reducing their impact on your daily life.

Emotional awareness is a skill that takes time and practice to develop. Be patient with yourself and celebrate small victories along the way. Each step you take towards understanding your emotions brings you closer to a more balanced and fulfilling life.

CHAPTER 4

Coping with Intense Emotion

Emotions can be like a storm, unpredictable and overwhelming. For those with Borderline Personality Disorder (BPD), these emotional storms can feel even more intense and difficult to manage. But there's hope. By learning practical strategies and grounding techniques, you can navigate these emotional challenges and find a sense of calm and control.

Practical Strategies for Managing Emotional Intensity

Intense emotions can be challenging to handle, but with the right strategies, you can manage them effectively. Here are some practical techniques to help you cope with emotional intensity:

1. Identify and Label Your Emotions:

The first step in managing intense emotions is to identify and label them. When you feel overwhelmed, take a moment to pause and ask yourself what you are feeling. Are you angry, sad, anxious, or scared? Naming your emotions can help you gain control over them. For example, saying to yourself, "I am feeling angry because of the argument I had with my friend," helps you understand the root cause of your emotions and gives you a starting point for addressing them.

2. Use the "STOP" Skill:

The "**STOP**" skill is a powerful tool for managing emotional intensity. It stands for:

- **Stop:** Pause whatever you are doing to break the cycle of emotional escalation.

- **Take a step back:** Physically or mentally step away from the situation to gain perspective.

- **Observe:** Notice what is happening around you and within you. What are you thinking, feeling, and sensing in your body?

- **Proceed mindfully:** Choose a thoughtful response instead of reacting impulsively.

3. Engage in Opposite Action:

When you experience an intense emotion, it can be helpful to engage in an activity that is opposite to what you are feeling. For example, if you are feeling sad and withdrawn, try doing something active and engaging, like going for a walk or calling a friend. This technique can help shift your emotional state and prevent you from getting stuck in negative feelings.

4. Practice Self-Compassion:

Intense emotions can often lead to self-criticism and negative self-talk. Instead, practice self-compassion by treating yourself with the same kindness and understanding that you would offer to a friend. Remind yourself that it is okay to feel intense emotions and that you are doing your best to manage them. This approach can help reduce the intensity of your emotions and promote a more balanced perspective.

5. Use Distraction Techniques:

Distraction can be a useful tool for managing emotional intensity. Engage in activities that capture your attention and divert your focus away from your emotions. This could include watching a movie, reading a book, playing a game, or engaging in a hobby. Distraction can provide temporary relief and give you time to calm down before addressing the underlying issue.

Grounding Techniques and Self-Soothing Methods

Grounding techniques and self-soothing methods are essential tools for managing intense emotions. These practices help you stay connected to the present moment and provide comfort during emotional distress.

1. Grounding Techniques:

<u>5-4-3-2-1 Technique:</u>

This grounding exercise helps you connect with your surroundings and distract yourself from overwhelming emotions. Identify:

- 5 things you can see

- 4 things you can touch

- 3 things you can hear

- 2 things you can smell

- 1 thing you can taste

By focusing on your senses, you can bring yourself back to the present moment and reduce the intensity of your emotions.

Deep Breathing:

Deep breathing is a simple yet effective grounding technique. Sit or lie down in a comfortable position, close your eyes, and take slow, deep breaths. Inhale deeply through your nose, hold the breath for a few seconds, and then exhale slowly through your mouth. Repeat this process several times until you feel calmer. Deep breathing helps activate the body's relaxation response, reducing stress and anxiety.

Body Scan:

A body scan involves paying attention to different parts of your body, from head to toe. Sit or lie down comfortably and slowly bring your focus to each part of your body, starting with your toes and moving up to your head. Notice any sensations, tension, or discomfort. This technique can help you become more aware of your physical state and bring you back to the present moment.

2. Self-Soothing Methods:

<u>Create a Comfort Kit:</u>

A comfort kit is a collection of items that provide you with comfort and relaxation during times of distress. This could include a soft blanket, a favorite book, soothing music, scented candles, or a stress ball. Having a comfort kit readily available can help you self-soothe when you are feeling overwhelmed.

<u>Engage Your Senses:</u>

Using your senses can be a powerful way to soothe yourself. Listen to calming music, light a scented candle, take a warm bath, or wrap yourself in a cozy blanket. Engaging your senses helps distract your mind and provides physical comfort.

Practice Mindfulness:

Mindfulness involves paying attention to the present moment without judgment. Practice mindfulness by focusing on your breath, observing your thoughts and feelings without reacting to them, or engaging in mindful activities such as coloring or gardening. Mindfulness can help you stay grounded and reduce the impact of intense emotions.

Use Positive Affirmations:

Positive affirmations are statements that promote self-acceptance and encourage positive thinking. Create a list of affirmations that resonate with you, such as "I am strong and capable," "I can handle this," or "I am worthy of love and respect." Repeat these affirmations to yourself during times of distress to boost your confidence and self-worth.

Managing intense emotions is a skill that requires practice and patience. By using practical strategies like identifying and labeling your emotions, engaging in opposite action, and practicing self-compassion, you can take control of your emotional responses. Grounding techniques and self-soothing methods, such as the 5-4-3-2-1 technique, deep breathing, and creating a comfort kit, can provide immediate relief and help you stay connected to the present moment.

It is okay to feel intense emotions, and it is possible to manage them effectively. By incorporating these strategies into your daily routine, you can build emotional resilience and navigate the challenges of BPD with confidence. Each step you take towards managing your emotions brings you closer to a more balanced and fulfilling life. Stay committed to this journey, and know that you have the power to thrive despite the challenges of BPD.

CHAPTER 5

Effective Communication

Imagine you're in the middle of a heated argument with a loved one. Your heart is pounding, your thoughts are racing, and you feel a surge of intense emotions threatening to take over. For many people with Borderline Personality Disorder (BPD), situations like this can feel overwhelming and difficult to navigate. However, learning to communicate effectively can transform these moments of conflict into opportunities for understanding and connection.

Effective communication involves expressing your emotions constructively and setting clear boundaries.

Expressing Emotions Constructively

One of the biggest challenges for individuals with BPD is expressing emotions in a way that is clear, direct, and respectful. Intense emotions can sometimes lead to outbursts or withdrawal, which can strain relationships. Here are some strategies to help you express your emotions constructively:

First, it's important to understand and articulate what you're feeling. When you experience strong emotions, take a moment to pause and reflect on what you're feeling and why. Instead of reacting impulsively, try to identify the specific emotion you're experiencing. For example, if you're feeling angry, ask yourself if there is underlying sadness, fear, or frustration contributing to that anger. Once you have a clearer understanding of your emotions, you can express them more effectively.

When you're ready to communicate, use "I" statements to express your feelings. This approach focuses on your own experience rather than blaming or accusing the other person. For instance, instead of saying, "You never listen to me," you could say, "I feel unheard when I try to share my thoughts." This subtle shift in language can reduce defensiveness and open up a more constructive dialogue.

Timing and setting are also crucial when it comes to expressing emotions. Choose a time when both you and the other person are calm and receptive. Trying to communicate during a heated moment can escalate the conflict. Additionally, find a quiet, private space where you can talk without distractions. This creates an environment where both parties can focus on the conversation and listen to each other.

Listening is an equally important part of effective communication. When the other person responds, make a conscious effort to listen actively. This means giving them your full attention, acknowledging their feelings, and avoiding interrupting. Reflect back what you've heard by summarizing their points, which shows that you understand and validates their perspective.

Assertiveness Training and Boundary Setting

Assertiveness is the ability to express your thoughts, feelings, and needs openly and respectfully, without being passive or aggressive. For individuals with BPD, developing assertiveness can be a transformative skill that enhances self-respect and strengthens relationships.

To start, it's helpful to understand the difference between assertiveness, passivity, and aggression. Passive communication involves not expressing your needs or allowing others to take advantage of you. Aggressive communication, on the other hand, involves expressing your needs in a hostile or disrespectful manner. Assertiveness strikes a balance by being honest and direct while respecting the rights and feelings of others.

One effective way to practice assertiveness is through role-playing. Imagine a scenario where you need to assert yourself, such as asking a friend to respect your time or expressing your discomfort with a colleague's behavior. Practice what you would say and how you would say it. Focus on using calm, clear, and respectful language. Role-playing can help you build confidence and prepare for real-life situations.

Setting boundaries is a crucial aspect of assertiveness. Boundaries define what is acceptable and unacceptable behavior from others. They protect your emotional well-being and ensure that your needs are met. To set boundaries effectively, it's important to be clear and specific about what you need. For example, if you need alone time to recharge, you might say, "I need some time to myself after work. I'll be available to talk in an hour."

Communicating boundaries requires consistency and follow-through. If someone crosses your boundaries, calmly remind them of your needs and the consequences of not respecting them. For instance, you might say, "I need my personal space respected. If it continues to be ignored, I'll need to take a step back from our interactions for a while." Consistency helps others understand that your boundaries are important and must be respected.

Effective communication, assertiveness, and boundary setting are interconnected skills that can significantly improve your relationships and emotional health. By expressing your emotions constructively, you can reduce misunderstandings and conflicts. Using "I" statements, choosing the right time and setting, and practicing active listening are key strategies for clear and respectful communication.

Developing assertiveness and setting boundaries involves understanding your needs and communicating them confidently and respectfully. Role-playing scenarios and being consistent in your boundaries can help you build these skills over time. Remember, being assertive doesn't mean being selfish; it means valuing yourself and your needs while also respecting others.

As you continue to practice these skills, you'll likely notice a positive shift in your interactions and relationships. Communication is a journey, and each step you take brings you closer to more meaningful and fulfilling connections. Embrace this journey with patience and compassion for yourself, knowing that every effort you make is a step towards a healthier, more balanced life.

PART III

Building Resilience

CHAPTER 6

Developing a Growth Mindset

I had always struggled with Borderline Personality Disorder (BPD) for most of my life. Every setback felt like a catastrophe, and I often doubted my ability to improve or succeed. But one day, I discovered the concept of a growth mindset, and it transformed my life. Through cultivating a positive and proactive mindset, I found resilience and adaptability I never knew I had. This chapter is about how you, too, can develop a growth mindset and harness its power to thrive despite the challenges of BPD.

The Importance of a Positive and Proactive Mindset

A growth mindset is the belief that your abilities, intelligence, and talents can be developed over time through dedication and hard work. It contrasts with a fixed mindset, which assumes that these qualities are static and unchangeable. Adopting a growth mindset is crucial for individuals with BPD because it opens the door to personal growth and resilience.

Imagine viewing each challenge not as a threat but as an opportunity to learn and grow. This shift in perspective can significantly reduce the intensity of emotional reactions and build confidence in your ability to handle life's ups and downs. With a growth mindset, you start to see failures not as defining moments but as stepping stones to success.

For me, embracing a growth mindset meant changing my internal dialogue. Instead of thinking, "I'll never get better at managing my emotions," I started telling myself, "I can learn and improve with practice and patience." This positive and proactive attitude gave me the motivation to seek out new strategies and skills for managing my BPD symptoms.

Strategies for Cultivating Resilience and Adaptability

Developing a growth mindset involves specific strategies that foster resilience and adaptability. These strategies can help you bounce back from setbacks and navigate the challenges of BPD with greater ease and confidence.

One of the first steps is to recognize and challenge your negative self-talk. Pay attention to the critical inner voice that says you're not good enough or that you'll never change. When you catch yourself thinking this way, pause and reframe those thoughts. For example, if you think, "I can't handle this situation," reframe it to, "This situation is difficult, but I can find ways to manage it." This shift in thinking helps you approach challenges with a problem-solving mindset rather than a defeatist attitude.

I personally found that setting realistic, achievable goals was another key to developing resilience. Instead of overwhelming myself with the pressure to make drastic changes overnight, I set small, manageable goals. For instance, I started by focusing on practicing mindfulness for five minutes each day. Gradually, I increased the duration and incorporated more mindfulness techniques into my daily routine. Celebrating these small victories helped build my confidence and reinforced my growth mindset.

Another important strategy is to embrace the process of learning and growth. Understand that progress is not always linear, and setbacks are a natural part of the journey. When I faced setbacks, I reminded myself that these were opportunities to learn and improve. I viewed mistakes as valuable feedback rather than failures. This perspective allowed me to stay resilient and adaptable, even when things didn't go as planned.

Surrounding yourself with a supportive community can also enhance your growth mindset. Connect with others who encourage and believe in your potential. Share your experiences and learn from theirs. I joined a support group for individuals with BPD, where I found encouragement, advice, and understanding from others who were on similar journeys. This sense of community helped me feel less alone and more motivated to continue working on my personal growth.

Cultivating resilience and adaptability also involves practicing self-compassion. Be kind to yourself when things don't go as expected. Instead of berating yourself for perceived failures, offer yourself the same compassion you would extend to a friend. Recognize that everyone makes mistakes and that you are doing your best. I learned to treat myself with gentle understanding, which reduced my self-critical tendencies and allowed me to recover more quickly from setbacks.

Developing a growth mindset is a powerful tool for thriving with BPD. By adopting a positive and proactive mindset, you can transform challenges into opportunities for growth and build resilience and adaptability. Remember my journey: how I shifted my internal dialogue, set achievable goals, embraced the learning process, and sought support from a community. You can do the same.

Start by challenging your negative self-talk and reframing your thoughts. Set small, realistic goals and celebrate your progress along the way. Embrace setbacks as learning opportunities and practice self-compassion. Surround yourself with supportive individuals who believe in your potential.

As you cultivate a growth mindset, you'll find that your ability to manage BPD symptoms improves, and your confidence grows. You'll become more resilient, adaptable, and capable of facing life's challenges head-on. Remember, developing a growth mindset is a journey, and each step you take brings you closer to a more fulfilling and empowered life. Keep believing in your potential, and know that you have the strength to thrive despite the challenges of BPD.

CHAPTER 7

Self-Compassion and Self-Care

Still using myself as a case study, I was a person with Borderline Personality Disorder (BPD) who, for years, struggled with intense self-criticism and feelings of worthlessness. Every mistake felt like a personal failure, and the emotional turmoil was relentless. But my journey took a positive turn when they discovered the power of self-compassion and self-care.

The Significance of Self-Compassion in Healing

Self-compassion involves treating yourself with the same kindness, understanding, and support that you would offer to a friend. For individuals with BPD, this can be a radical shift, as the disorder often fuels harsh self-judgment and criticism. Embracing self-compassion is not about excusing harmful behavior or avoiding responsibility; it's about acknowledging your struggles with empathy and a desire to improve.

When I first encountered the idea of self-compassion, it felt foreign. They were used to beating themselves up over every perceived failure. But as they began to practice self-compassion, they noticed a significant change. Instead of spiraling into shame and self-loathing, I started to approach their emotions with curiosity and kindness. They would say to themselves, "It's okay to feel this way. I'm doing my best, and I deserve understanding and care."

One of the key aspects of self-compassion is mindfulness, which involves being present with your emotions without judgment. For me, this meant acknowledging their pain without trying to suppress or deny it. They learned to sit with their feelings, recognizing them as part of the human experience rather than a personal flaw. This mindful approach allowed me to process their emotions more effectively and reduced the intensity of their emotional reactions.

Another crucial element of self-compassion is common humanity. Understanding that suffering and imperfection are part of the shared human experience helps you realize that you are not alone in your struggles. I found comfort in knowing that others also faced similar challenges and that it was okay to seek support. This sense of connection reduced feelings of isolation and increased their willingness to reach out for help when needed.

Practical Self-Care Routines and Habits

Self-care is the practice of taking intentional actions to maintain and improve your physical, mental, and emotional health. It's not a one-size-fits-all solution but rather a personalized approach to nurturing yourself. For me, developing practical self-care routines and habits was a game-changer in managing their BPD symptoms and enhancing their overall well-being.

A foundational aspect of self-care is establishing a daily routine that includes activities promoting health and relaxation. I started by incorporating simple practices into their day, such as:

1. Morning Mindfulness:

Each morning, I set aside 10 minutes for mindfulness meditation. Sitting quietly and focusing on their breath helped them start the day with a calm and centered mind. This practice reduced morning anxiety and set a positive tone for the rest of the day.

2. Physical Activity:

Regular exercise became a cornerstone of my self-care routine. Whether it was a brisk walk, yoga session, or dance class, physical activity helped release pent-up energy and improved their mood. I found that even short bursts of exercise could significantly reduce stress and enhance their sense of well-being.

3. Nutritious Eating:

I made a conscious effort to nourish their body with healthy foods. They discovered that balanced meals with plenty of fruits, vegetables, and whole grains provided sustained energy and improved their mental clarity. Staying hydrated and limiting caffeine and sugar intake also made a noticeable difference in their mood stability.

4. Creative Expression:

Engaging in creative activities like painting, writing, or playing music became an essential part of my self-care. These outlets allowed them to express their emotions constructively and provided a sense of accomplishment and joy. I noticed that creativity helped them process complex feelings and reduced emotional overwhelm.

5. Social Connection:

Building and maintaining supportive relationships were vital for my emotional health. They made it a point to connect with friends and loved ones regularly, whether through phone calls, video chats, or in-person visits. Sharing experiences and receiving emotional support from others helped me feel understood and less alone.

6. Rest and Relaxation:

Recognizing the importance of rest, I prioritized getting enough sleep each night. They established a relaxing bedtime routine, which included activities like reading, listening to calming music, or taking a warm bath. Adequate sleep significantly improved their mood and ability to cope with daily stresses.

7. Setting Boundaries:

Learning to set and maintain healthy boundaries was crucial for my self-care. They practiced saying no to activities or commitments that felt overwhelming and made time for themselves. This practice helped reduce feelings of burnout and ensured they had the energy to focus on their well-being.

Self-compassion and self-care are not just concepts; they are transformative practices that can significantly enhance your ability to manage BPD and improve your quality of life. By treating yourself with kindness and understanding, as I did, you can break the cycle of self-criticism and embrace a more nurturing approach to your emotional health.

Incorporating practical self-care routines into your daily life can create a foundation of stability and resilience. Start with small, manageable changes, and gradually build habits that support your physical, mental, and emotional well-being. Remember, self-care is a personal journey, and it's important to find what works best for you.

CHAPTER 8

Building Healthy Relationships

Building healthy relationships is a cornerstone of emotional well-being and resilience, especially for individuals with Borderline Personality Disorder (BPD). Relationships can either uplift you or drain you, depending on their nature. In this chapter, we'll explore how to identify toxic relationships and set necessary boundaries while focusing on nurturing supportive and positive connections.

Identifying Toxic Relationships and Setting Boundaries

Toxic relationships are those that consistently undermine your well-being and self-worth. Recognizing these relationships is the first step toward fostering a healthier social environment. Here are some characteristics of toxic relationships:

- **Consistent Negativity:** If someone constantly criticizes, belittles, or invalidates your feelings, this is a red flag. Healthy relationships should involve mutual respect and constructive support.

- **Manipulation and Control:** Toxic individuals often try to control your actions, thoughts, or feelings. They may use guilt, shame, or fear to manipulate you into doing what they want.

- **Lack of Empathy:** If a person shows little to no understanding or concern for your feelings and needs, it can create an emotionally draining environment.

- **Volatility:** Relationships marked by frequent arguments, dramatic mood swings, or passive-aggressive behavior can be exhausting and damaging.

Recognizing these signs is crucial. Once you've identified a toxic relationship, setting boundaries is the next important step. Boundaries are limits you set to protect your well-being and personal space. Here's how you can effectively set and maintain boundaries:

1. Be Clear and Specific: Clearly communicate your boundaries to the other person. Instead of vague statements, be specific about what behaviors are unacceptable and what you need from the relationship. For example, say, "I need you to speak to me respectfully and avoid raising your voice during our conversations."

2. Be Consistent: Consistency is key to enforcing boundaries. If you set a boundary but do not follow through, it sends a message that the boundary is not serious. Consistently uphold your limits to ensure they are respected.

3. Use "I" Statements: When discussing boundaries, use "I" statements to focus on your feelings and needs rather than blaming the other person. For instance, say, "I feel uncomfortable when you criticize me in public. I need you to address concerns privately."

4. Stay Calm and Composed: It's essential to remain calm and composed when setting boundaries. Emotional outbursts can escalate conflicts and make it harder to communicate effectively.

5. Be Prepared for Resistance: Some people may resist or challenge your boundaries. Stand firm and reiterate your needs calmly. Remember, setting boundaries is about protecting your well-being, not about controlling others.

Nurturing Supportive and Positive Connections

While it's vital to identify and manage toxic relationships, it's equally important to nurture supportive and positive connections. Positive relationships can provide emotional support, enhance your sense of belonging, and improve your overall well-being. Here's how to cultivate and maintain healthy relationships:

1. Choose Supportive Individuals: Surround yourself with people who respect you, understand your needs, and encourage your growth. These individuals are empathetic, reliable, and genuinely care about your well-being.

2. Communicate Openly: Open and honest communication is the foundation of any healthy relationship. Share your thoughts, feelings, and needs with your friends and loved ones. Encourage them to do the same. This mutual sharing fosters trust and understanding.

3. Practice Active Listening: Listening is as important as speaking in a relationship. When someone is talking to you, give them your full attention. Avoid interrupting and show empathy by acknowledging their feelings. Active listening shows that you value and respect the other person's perspective.

4. Show Appreciation: Regularly express gratitude and appreciation for the people in your life. Small gestures, like saying thank you or acknowledging their support, can strengthen your bond and make others feel valued.

5. Spend Quality Time: Make an effort to spend quality time with supportive individuals. Engage in activities that you both enjoy, whether it's going for a walk, having a coffee, or simply talking. Shared experiences create lasting memories and deepen your connection.

6. Be Supportive: Healthy relationships are reciprocal. Be there for your friends and loved ones during their times of need. Offer a listening ear, a helping hand, or words of encouragement. Being supportive not only strengthens your relationship but also builds a sense of mutual trust and reliability.

7. Respect Differences: Every person is unique, and respecting differences is crucial for a healthy relationship. Accept that others may have different opinions, values, and ways of doing things. Respecting these differences fosters a harmonious and accepting environment.

8. Resolve Conflicts Constructively: Conflicts are a natural part of any relationship. What matters is how you handle them. Approach conflicts with a problem-solving mindset rather than a confrontational one. Focus on finding solutions that work for both parties rather than winning the argument.

9. Seek Professional Help if Needed: Sometimes, building and maintaining healthy relationships can be challenging, especially if you have past experiences that affect your interactions. Don't hesitate to seek the help of a therapist or counselor. They can provide valuable insights and strategies for improving your relationships.

Building healthy relationships involves both identifying and managing toxic connections and nurturing supportive ones. By setting clear boundaries, communicating openly, and practicing empathy and respect, you can create a network of relationships that enhance your emotional well-being and support your journey with BPD. Remember, you deserve relationships that uplift and empower you. Keep these strategies in mind as you navigate your social interactions, and you will find that healthy, positive relationships are within your reach.

PART IV

Living a Fulfilling Life

CHAPTER 9

Finding Purpose and Meaning

Finding purpose and meaning in life is essential for living a fulfilling life, especially when managing Borderline Personality Disorder (BPD). A sense of purpose can provide direction, motivation, and resilience, helping you navigate the complexities of your emotions and experiences.

Techniques for Discovering Personal Passions and Goals

Discovering your passions and goals begins with self-exploration and reflection. Here are some techniques to help you uncover what truly matters to you:

1. Reflect on Past Joys and Successes: Think about the activities and experiences that have brought you the most joy and satisfaction in the past. What were you doing? Who were you with? Why did those moments stand out? This reflection can provide valuable clues about your passions.

2. Identify Your Core Values: Core values are the principles that guide your decisions and actions. They reflect what is most important to you. Spend some time thinking about your core values. Is it creativity, helping others, learning, or something else? Understanding your core values can help you align your passions with your goals.

3. Experiment and Explore: Don't be afraid to try new things. Take up a new hobby, volunteer for a cause you care about, or join a club. Experimenting with different activities can help you discover what resonates with you and what you're passionate about.

4. Listen to Your Intuition: Sometimes, your gut feeling or intuition can guide you toward your passions. Pay attention to what excites you or what you feel drawn to, even if it doesn't make logical sense initially.

5. Seek Feedback from Others: Sometimes, others can see our strengths and passions more clearly than we can. Ask friends, family, or colleagues what they think you're good at and what they've noticed you enjoy doing. Their insights can provide valuable perspectives.

6. Journal and Reflect: Writing down your thoughts, feelings, and experiences can help you gain clarity. Journaling about what you enjoy, what you're curious about, and what you want to achieve can uncover hidden passions and goals.

7. Set Aside Time for Introspection: Regularly setting aside quiet time for introspection can help you connect with your inner self. Meditate, take long walks, or simply sit in silence and reflect on your life, your desires, and your aspirations.

Once you've identified your passions and goals, it's important to align them with your daily actions. This alignment ensures that your everyday life contributes to your long-term aspirations, creating a sense of purpose and fulfillment.

Aligning Daily Actions with Long-Term Aspirations

Aligning your daily actions with your long-term goals involves creating a roadmap that integrates your passions into your everyday life. Here's how you can do it:

1. Set Clear and Achievable Goals: Break down your long-term aspirations into smaller, manageable goals. These goals should be specific, measurable, attainable, relevant, and time-bound **(SMART).** For instance, if your long-term goal is to become a skilled painter, a short-term goal could be to complete a painting course within three months.

2. Create a Vision Board: Visualizing your goals can make them feel more tangible and motivate you to take action. Create a vision board with images, quotes, and symbols that represent your passions and aspirations. Place it somewhere you'll see daily as a constant reminder of your purpose.

3. Develop a Daily Routine: Incorporate activities that align with your passions into your daily routine. If your goal is to write a novel, set aside a specific time each day for writing. Consistency is key to making progress and staying connected to your goals.

4. Prioritize Self-Care: Taking care of your mental, emotional, and physical well-being is essential for staying motivated and focused. Ensure that your routine includes time for rest, relaxation, and activities that recharge you. This balance will help you maintain the energy and enthusiasm needed to pursue your passions.

5. Stay Flexible and Adaptable: Life is unpredictable, and sometimes plans change. Stay flexible and adaptable, allowing yourself to adjust your goals and actions as needed. This flexibility ensures that you remain aligned with your purpose, even when circumstances shift.

6. Celebrate Small Wins: Acknowledge and celebrate your progress, no matter how small. Recognizing your achievements, even the minor ones, can boost your motivation and reinforce your commitment to your goals.

7. Seek Support and Accountability: Share your goals with supportive friends, family, or a mentor. Having someone to encourage you and hold you accountable can make a significant difference in your journey. They can provide motivation, guidance, and a different perspective when needed.

8. Reflect and Reassess Regularly: Periodically take time to reflect on your progress and reassess your goals. Are your daily actions still aligned with your long-term aspirations? Are your goals still meaningful to you? This reflection helps you stay on track and make necessary adjustments.

Finding purpose and meaning in life is a powerful antidote to the challenges of BPD. By discovering your personal passions and aligning your daily actions with your long-term goals, you can create a life filled with direction, motivation, and fulfillment. Remember, this journey is deeply personal and unique to you. Take the time to explore, experiment, and reflect on what truly matters to you.

CHAPTER 10
Setting and Achieving Goals

Setting and achieving goals is a critical skill, especially for those managing Borderline Personality Disorder (BPD). Goals give you a sense of direction and purpose, helping you navigate through the ups and downs of life with greater clarity and determination. In this chapter, we'll explore the **SMART** goal-setting framework, providing you with a structured approach to defining and reaching your objectives. Additionally, we'll delve into strategies for overcoming obstacles and maintaining motivation, ensuring that your path to success remains steady and fulfilling.

The SMART Goal-Setting Framework

Setting goals isn't just about deciding what you want to achieve; it's about creating a clear, actionable plan that guides you towards your desired outcome. The **SMART** framework is an excellent tool for this, as it ensures that your goals are well-defined and attainable. **SMART** stands for Specific, Measurable, Achievable, Relevant, and Time-bound.

1. Specific: Your goal should be clear and specific. Vague goals are hard to achieve because they don't provide a clear direction. Instead of saying, "I want to be healthier," specify what that means to you. For example, "I want to exercise for 30 minutes every day."

2. Measurable: A measurable goal allows you to track your progress and stay motivated. It answers questions like "How much?" or "How many?" and

"How will I know when it is accomplished?" Using the previous example, you could measure your progress by keeping a daily exercise log.

3. Achievable: Your goal should be realistic and attainable to be successful. While it's good to challenge yourself, setting a goal that is too ambitious can lead to frustration and disappointment. Assess your current situation and set a goal that stretches your abilities but remains feasible.

4. Relevant: Your goal should matter to you and align with your other life objectives. Ensure that it's something you genuinely want to achieve and that it's relevant to your broader aspirations. For instance, exercising daily should align with your broader goal of improving your overall health.

5. Time-bound: Every goal needs a target date, so you have a deadline to focus on and something to work towards. This part of the **SMART** goal framework helps to prevent everyday tasks from taking priority over your longer-term goals. For example, "I want to exercise for 30 minutes every day for the next three months."

Overcoming Obstacles and Maintaining Motivation

Even with a well-defined goal, you will inevitably encounter obstacles. These challenges can derail your progress if not managed effectively. Here's how to overcome these obstacles and maintain your motivation throughout your goal-setting journey:

1. Anticipate Challenges: Before you even start working towards your goal, take some time to anticipate potential challenges. What obstacles might you encounter? What could go wrong? By identifying potential issues ahead of time, you can create contingency plans to address them.

2. Develop a Resilience Mindset: Resilience is your ability to bounce back from setbacks. Cultivate a mindset that views obstacles as opportunities for growth rather than insurmountable barriers. Remind yourself that setbacks are a natural part of any journey and can provide valuable learning experiences.

3. Break Down Goals: Large goals can feel overwhelming, making it easy to lose motivation. Break your goals into smaller, more manageable tasks. This approach not only makes your goal seem more attainable but also allows you to celebrate small victories along the way.

4. Stay Flexible: Life is unpredictable, and sometimes you'll need to adjust your goals or your approach. Stay flexible and open to change. If something isn't working, don't be afraid to reassess and pivot. Flexibility can help you stay on track even when things don't go as planned.

5. Use Positive Reinforcement: Reward yourself for making progress, no matter how small. Positive reinforcement can boost your motivation and keep you moving forward. Rewards don't have to be extravagant; even small treats or moments of relaxation can serve as effective incentives.

6. Build a Support System: Surround yourself with supportive people who can encourage you and hold you accountable. Share your goals with friends, family, or a support group. Their encouragement and feedback can be invaluable, especially during challenging times.

7. Visualize Success: Visualization can be a powerful motivational tool. Spend time imagining yourself achieving your goal. What does success look like? How will you feel once you've accomplished it? This mental rehearsal can boost your confidence and keep you focused on your objective.

8. Stay Connected to Your "Why": Always keep the reason behind your goal at the forefront of your mind. Why did you set this goal in the first place? What will achieving it mean for you and your life? Staying connected to your "why" can reignite your motivation when you feel like giving up.

Setting and achieving goals is not just about the end result; it's about the journey and the growth you experience along the way. By using the **SMART** framework, you can create clear, actionable goals that guide you toward success. Remember to anticipate challenges, stay flexible, and connect with your support system to maintain your motivation.

Your goals are within reach, and with determination and perseverance, you can achieve them and live a fulfilling, purpose-driven life.

CHAPTER 11

Thriving in Everyday Life

Imagine waking up each morning with a sense of purpose and calm, ready to tackle whatever the day brings. This isn't just a distant dream but a reality you can achieve by integrating the strategies you've learned into your daily routines. Picture yourself living a life where managing Borderline Personality Disorder (BPD) is part of your daily rhythm, allowing you to thrive despite the challenges. This chapter will guide you on how to weave these strategies into your everyday life, maintain your progress, and celebrate your achievements.

Integrating the Strategies into Daily Routines

Like I mentioned earlier in this book, I struggled with BPD for years. But then, upon recovering I start my day by waking up to the gentle sound of my alarm, avoiding the jarring beeps that used to set a stressful tone. I take a few moments to breathe deeply and set a positive intention for the day. This small practice, learned from my journey, has become a cornerstone of my morning routine.

As I get ready for work, I incorporate mindfulness into my activities. While brushing my teeth or making my bed, I focus on the sensations and movements, grounding myself in the present moment. This practice helps me stay centered and reduces the anxiety that used to cloud my mornings.

At breakfast, I take time to plan my meals, ensuring I include nutritious options that support my mental well-being. I learned that balanced nutrition plays a vital role in stabilizing my mood and energy levels. Eating mindfully, I avoid distractions and enjoy my food, which keeps me present and calm.

Throughout my workday, I use brief mindfulness breaks to stay balanced. When I feel emotions rising, I practice deep breathing exercises or a quick body scan. These techniques help me manage my emotions effectively and prevent them from overwhelming me.

I also schedule time for self-care. After work, I dedicate an hour to activities that rejuvenate me, like reading, gardening, or doing yoga. These moments of self-care are non-negotiable, as they help me recharge and maintain my emotional balance.

In my interactions, I make sure I practice assertive communication. I make use of the **"I"** statement to express my needs and feelings clearly, avoiding the misunderstandings that used to lead to conflict. Setting boundaries has become a natural part of my relationships, ensuring that I feel respected and understood.

Every evening, I reflect on my day, noting what went well and what I can improve. I journal my thoughts, which helps me process my experiences and set intentions for the next day. This reflection has become a valuable tool for my growth and self-awareness.

Maintaining Progress and Celebrating Achievements

Let's look at how I maintained progress and celebrated my achievements. I set short-term goals that are manageable and tangible. For instance, I might aim to practice mindfulness for five minutes every morning for a week. Achieving this small goal boosts my confidence and motivates me to set new ones.

I also tend to track my progress in a journal, documenting my achievements and setbacks. This visual record helps me see how far I've come and provides a source of motivation on tougher days. I acknowledge my progress, no matter how small, and use it as a foundation for further growth.

Celebrating small wins is a big part of my strategy. When I successfully manage a stressful situation or maintain my self-care routine for a week, I reward myself with something enjoyable, like a favorite treat or a relaxing bath. These rewards reinforce my positive behaviors and keep me motivated.

I stay flexible and adapt my strategies as needed. If a particular approach isn't working, I don't hesitate to try something new. This flexibility ensures that my methods remain effective and relevant to my evolving needs.

To stay connected to my purpose, I regularly remind myself of why I'm making these changes. I keep a list of my long-term goals and the positive impact they will have on my life. This connection to my deeper purpose sustains my motivation, especially during challenging times.

My support system plays a crucial role in my journey. I engage in regular check-ins with friends and family, sharing my progress and challenges. Their encouragement and feedback provide valuable support and accountability, helping me stay on track.

Through it all, I practice self-compassion. I recognize that setbacks are a natural part of the journey and don't beat myself up over them. Instead, I treat myself with kindness and understanding, which fuels my resilience and ability to bounce back.

My story illustrates how integrating strategies into daily routines, maintaining progress, and celebrating achievements can transform your life. Thriving with BPD is about persistence, self-awareness, and embracing the journey with compassion and dedication.

As you apply these principles to your own life, remember that every step, no matter how small, brings you closer to thriving in everyday life. Celebrate your progress, learn from setbacks, and remain committed to your path. With these practices, you can create a future filled with purpose, joy, and fulfillment.

Conclusion

As we come to the end of this journey together, it's essential to revisit the main strategies and takeaways we've explored. Understanding and managing Borderline Personality Disorder (BPD) is a multifaceted process, and each chapter in this book has provided you with tools to help you thrive.

You started by understanding what BPD is, including its symptoms, diagnostic criteria, and common misconceptions. From there, you delved into the science behind BPD, learning about the biological, psychological, and environmental factors that influence the disorder.

Managing emotions is crucial for those with BPD, and we discussed the importance of emotional awareness and coping with intense emotions. You learned practical strategies for identifying and understanding your emotions, as well as techniques like grounding and self-soothing to manage emotional intensity effectively.

Communication is another vital area, and we explored tools for expressing emotions constructively, assertiveness training, and boundary setting. Developing a growth mindset and practicing self-compassion and self-care were emphasized as foundational elements for building resilience and fostering emotional well-being.

Building healthy relationships is key to your overall happiness, and you learned how to identify toxic relationships, set boundaries, and nurture supportive connections. Living a fulfilling life involves finding purpose and meaning, setting and achieving goals, and integrating the strategies into your daily routines.

Finally, we focused on maintaining progress and celebrating achievements. The importance of reflecting on your journey, adapting your strategies, and practicing self-compassion were highlighted as essential components of ongoing growth and resilience.

Encouragement for the Future

As you move forward, remember that your journey with BPD is uniquely yours. There will be challenges and setbacks, but each step you take is a testament to your strength and determination. You have already demonstrated remarkable courage by seeking out strategies to improve your life and well-being.

Continue to apply the techniques you've learned, stay connected to your support system, and embrace each day with a sense of purpose and hope. Celebrate your progress, no matter how small, and be kind to yourself when things don't go as planned. Every effort you make brings you closer to a life of fulfillment and joy.

Your resilience and commitment to growth are inspiring. Believe in your ability to thrive, and let that belief guide you through the ups and downs of your journey. Remember, you are not alone—many others share your experiences and understand your struggles.

Your journey doesn't end here—it's just beginning. Continue to seek out knowledge, connect with others, and invest in your well-being. With the right tools, support, and mindset, you can navigate the complexities of BPD and build a life that is not only manageable but truly fulfilling.

Stay resilient, stay hopeful, and above all, stay kind to yourself. You have the power to thrive.